Great Teach

JENNY DENT
Illustrated by Christina Marsh

Spiritual teaching
for children series

4

THE WHITE EAGLE PUBLISHING TRUST
New Lands · Liss · Hampshire · England

Note for Parents

I dedicate this book to my beloved teacher, White Eagle, whose restatement of the spiritual truth of the Ancient Wisdom has been its source and inspiration.

I acknowledge with love and thanks what I owe to my mother, Joan Hodgson, for awakening my understanding of spiritual truth from earliest childhood, and for the example she set in starting our work with children in the White Eagle Lodge.

I should also like to thank Christina Marsh for her beautiful illustrations, Angela Blakstad for patiently typing the manuscript, and everyone else associated with its production.

This book is for you and your children to share and have fun with. How much they get out of it will depend a lot on YOU.

When should I start to teach my children about spiritual things?

Many parents have asked me, 'When should I start to teach my children about spiritual things?'. The answer is, now – the younger they are, the better. They will absorb so much from you and your attitude towards life, right from the start. This book is to help you give them an appreciation of spiritual things before materialism starts to fill their minds instead. It isn't intended to stop them deciding for themselves when they are grown up, but to provide some basic ideas which will help them now, and be a point from which they can later explore. It surely is every parent's duty to bring up their children in their own understanding of spiritual truth, and allow them later to choose their own path, when they have the maturity to do so.

How do I start?

When parents ask me, 'How do I start?', the simple answer is, 'Here, with these books', but also of course in every situation in daily life. Far better the occasional remark, such as, 'Let's all say thank you now to God, in our hearts, for the lovely world we live in' whilst out on a walk, than a long lecture every Sunday! Nature brings many opportunities to teach these things naturally, in the changing of the seasons, in birth and death, in our families and pets, and I hope these books will give you lots of ideas and thus help you even when they are shut away in a bookcase.

Our New Age children have such a great need for spiritual education, alongside their physical and mental training, that we must not fail them. As we go into the Aquarian Age, there will be even greater stimulation of the intellect, but this has to be balanced by an awakening of the heart to spiritual truth and understanding of the love of God and the brotherhood of all life.

The four initial titles in this series are GOD LOVES US ALL, WHERE IS HEAVEN?, THE GIANT JIGSAW – 'a spiritual law makes all the pieces fit' – and GREAT TEACHERS.

In these books, printed individually for greater flexibility of use within the family group, I cover the basic concepts most necessary to a child's growing understanding of spiritual truth.

It is preferable to work through them consecutively, but not essential, so you can pick out a particular topic (from any of the books) which answers a child's question and use the project page, meditation and prayer, without having read the previous sections.

The Explanatory Pages

(the left hand page of each section) I have written these as simply as I can in the words I would use to explain the subject to a child in the middle age range. Younger children may need them to be further simplified, which you can do as you read to them, or explain in your own words. Older children will read them for themselves and then, when you talk about them together, you can add more detail and discuss them further.

The important thing is that *you should participate* and share their discovery with them. Don't just give them the books and leave it at that. Parents who like to work to a routine may decide to take one section per day or week, to read and discuss before 'quiet time' and then lead into the MEDITATION and PRAYER for that section.

Meditation and Prayer

The meditations I have given are simple creative pictures based upon each theme. Learning meditation (at any age) needs regular practice, first to train the physical body and mind to keep still and to develop the ability to concentrate; and secondly by stages to close the physical senses to the outer world for the period of meditation and to become more and more aware of the still centre of God deep within the heart. This is the true purpose of meditation: it means seeking to become at one with God's light within our own hearts and with His Great Light which shines within all creation. Having made this God-contact we hope to become gradually illumined with God's light and God-like qualities, so that we can better serve our family of all creation. An 'outgiving' in service is essential, for our motive should not be concerned with spiritual progress for ourselves, but to become better channels for God's light to shine out into the world.

Many children take naturally to meditation, but all need much patience and loving help from their parents. It is a good idea to establish a meditation and prayer time in your children's routine from a very early age. Separate times for different age groups may be necessary as the very young ones can wriggle and disturb the older ones who are ready for a longer silence. Make it a happy family time when they know they have your full love and attention, so that it is something they look forward to. It is helpful to have a special 'prayer rug' or your yoga mat which you spread on the floor in your quiet room or bedroom, for these times. A simple cross-legged posture, or kneeling with feet tucked under, is good; and the hands may be lightly clasped in the lap, left cupped in right, or together in the traditional posture for prayer. I often tell children to think of their hands together like this as making the symbol of the little flame of God in their heart. Let them hold the meditation concentration for only a few moments at first, but gradually extend the time, then finish with the prayer.

Cut-out Project Pages

We have tried to design these to help children absorb spiritual truth while they enjoy an activity. Most children are quickly bored by sermon-type instruction and 'turn off', running away to find something else to do if they are allowed, so I hope they will enjoy these pages, which are linked to the theme of the explanatory page, meditation and prayer.

All pages have black-and-white illustrations designed for children to colour, but the project pages can be cut out and used separately by young children, to prevent their scribbling over the entire book!

Materials you will need:

A supply of thin card, e.g. empty cereal packets

A supply of paper fasteners. These are available from stationery shops and look like this: ▱◖

Glue for sticking paper to thin card

Round-ended scissors for children's use

Colouring pens or crayons

Several projects also require *a piece of elastic, string, stapler or a needle and thread.*

About my Teacher, White Eagle

My teacher, White Eagle, has helped me understand the truth and beauty in every religion and pathway to God, and he teaches the Ancient Wisdom with fresh insight for the new Aquarian Age. He says truth is like a great tree with many branches. Each pathway to God is like one little twig or branch. (It would be a mistake to think our twig was the most important part of the tree!)

I have known and loved White Eagle since childhood (and in many past lives, I believe). He did not come back to earth this time in a physical body himself, but inspired and worked through my grandmother, Grace Cooke. He is her spiritual guide and teacher, and had worked with her for many lives and trained her for this particular work. In 1936, following his guidance, she started a church (The White Eagle Lodge) to which people could come for healing, comfort, to learn the spiritual teaching of the Ancient Wisdom, and to give service to others.

White Eagle used the personality of an American Indian Chief of the Iroquois tribe (the name 'White Eagle' means a 'spiritual teacher) and we can learn much from the American Indians, and their way of life and spiritual knowledge.

But, now, in this New Age, a very special part of White Eagle's teaching is to help us use our inner light, the part of God, the Christ within the heart (the atman), in service to others, indeed to the whole of creation. Mankind is growing up and can learn now to work with his Creator to create a more perfect, more beautiful and more harmonious world. The six-pointed star symbol helps us do this; it helps stimulate the Christ light and the spark of God within our hearts. So picture it shining down on the whole world, helping awaken all mankind to the light . . . leading us into the new age of beauty and harmony.

GREAT TEACHERS

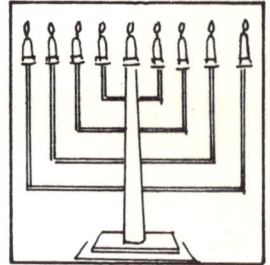

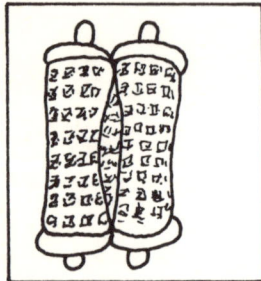

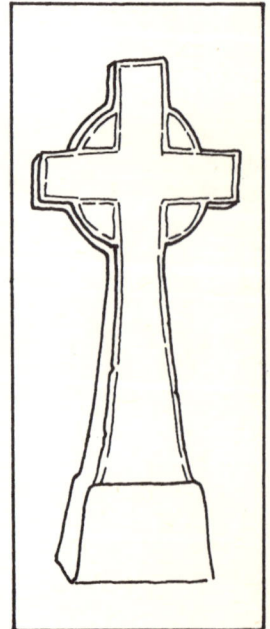

1. Great Teachers filled with God's Light

Our Creator, Father Mother God, loves all His children and knows that we need help during our lives on earth. One way help comes is from teachers who have learned the lessons which life on earth can teach, and are filled with God's light so that there is no separation between their higher shining self, and the lower self of every day (have a look at Book Two, WHERE IS HEAVEN?). They do not need to return to earth, but choose to do so to help those who are still struggling with their lower self and the lessons of earth life.

Throughout the history of life on earth, in all races, in all parts of the world, spiritual teachers have come to help the people in the way they most need at that time. Many are now known by the great religions which have grown from their teaching.

If you look deeply beneath the outer customs we see today (it is like an exciting treasure hunt), you will find that all the world religions have close links. This is because the truth they contain is a part of the 'Ancient Wisdom'. This is a name given to the truths about God and life which were originally brought to earth many thousands of years ago by wise, spiritual teachers.

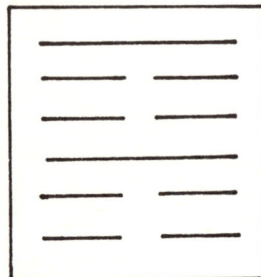

Great Teachers filled with God's Light

This picture for you to colour contains symbols or pictures linked with the great teachers and world religions. How many of them can you name? Look through the book for some answers.

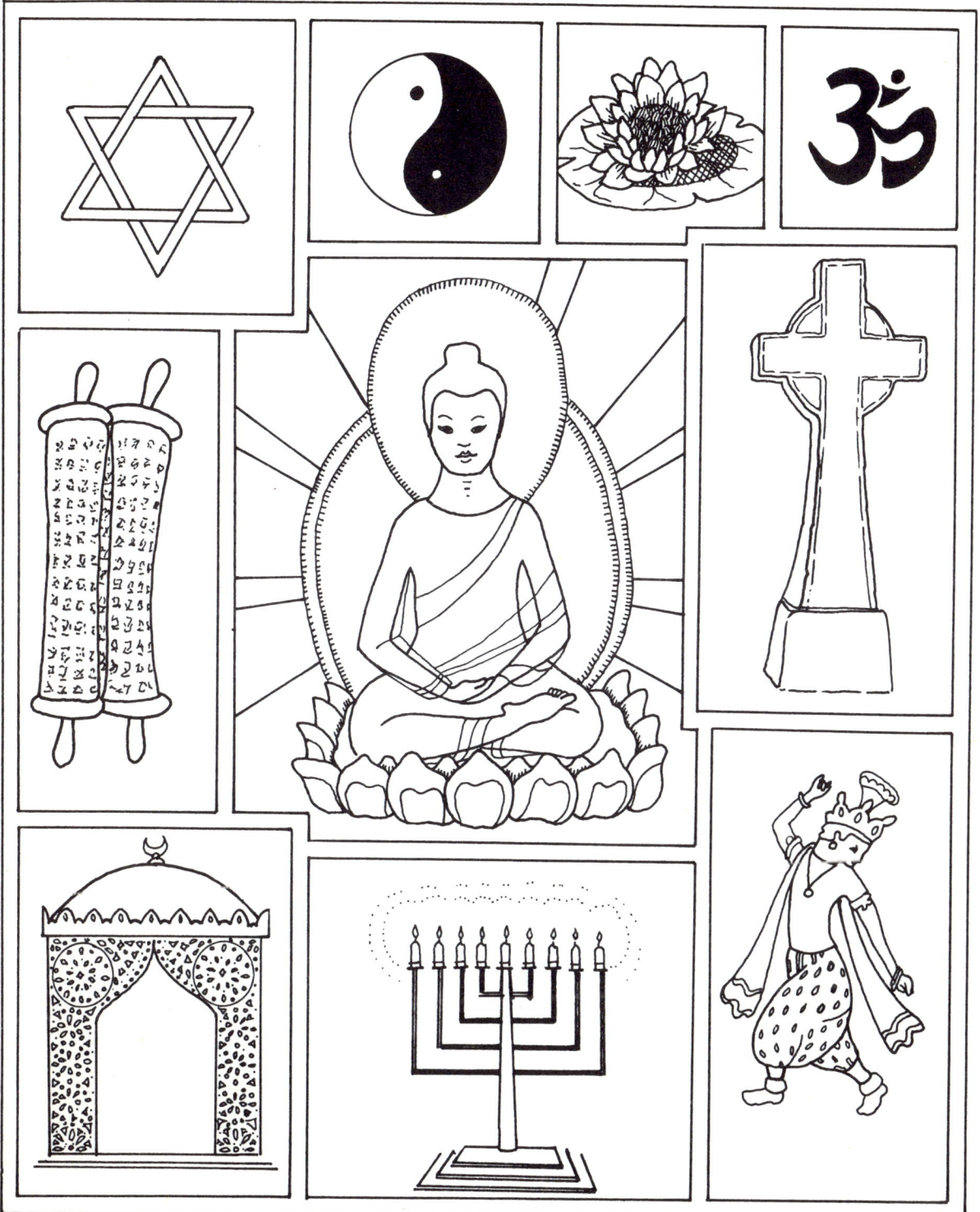

MAKE YOUR OWN 'WISDOM TELLER'

This is like a fortune teller but with great teachers' wise sayings. Follow the directions in the centre of the teller, and when you have practised opening and shutting it one way and the other, ask a friend to choose one of the four symbols on the outer flaps. Spell out the name, opening the teller one way for the first letter, the other way for the second, and so on. Show him the inside symbols that are displayed at the last opening. Now count the number shown in the same way. Finally get him to name one of the symbols shown, and open the teller right out to look under that one and read what is written.

CIRCLE

BUDDHA

∞ A 1

You yourself must make an effort. The Buddha (or teacher) can only show the way forward. BUDDHA

Keep on keeping on bravely on the path WHITE EAGLE

EAGLE

CROSS

TEN COMMANDMENTS

Honour thy father and thy mother. MOSES

YIN

YANG

LAO-TZU

He who speaks does not know. A kind word with forgiveness is better than charity followed by an insult. THE KORAN

TO MAKE THE WISDOM TELLER
1. Fold inwards along AA, BB, and open out again. Mark the centre where they cross
2. Fold *back* each corner to the centre along each line AB
3. Fold each of the new corners (A, A, B, B) *inwards* to the centre
4. Turn teller over and slip thumb and first finger of each hand into the four flaps. Pinch the corners together in the centre
5. Open to show first panels 2,3,6,7 and then 1,4,5,8 Practise doing this until you can do it fast

7
B
9

Let right deeds be the motive, not the fruit which comes from them. KRISHNA

FLUTE

2
B
3

A kind knows does not speak; he who does not know. THE KORAN

MOSQUE

STAR

HEXAGRAM

CHINESE PHILOSOPHER

An honest thought can move heaven and earth.

Love thy neighbour as thyself. JESUS

STABLE

LOTUS

5 A 4

6

Great Teachers filled with God's Light

MEDITATION

Picture the earth in darkness on a dark night. Then a great star shines in the sky and a beam of light reaches down to earth. The light touches the hearts of people in that part of the world and they look up from the dark earth to see, through the love of their teacher, the light and love of God.

Meditate on this picture and give thanks in your heart for all the teachers whose lives of service have given a great gift to humanity.

PRAYER

Dear Creator of All (called by some Allah, Jehovah, Brahman, Great Spirit, or God),

We thank you for your loving care and for the teachers you send to help lead us back to you and to understand more about our life on earth and in heaven. Please help us always to have open minds and to see the truth and beauty within every religion, for all are pathways leading to you.

Please help us too, to respect the beliefs and customs of others, even if they seem very strange to us. We know you love us all, no matter what religion we follow, and we are all part of your great family.

Amen.

2. Jesus

Jesus of Nazareth prepared for many lives for his incarnation as a world teacher, when he was able to bring a very special blessing to the world and the Christ Spirit, the Son of God, shone brightly through him.

After Jesus' death, his followers started to insist that only he was Son of God and that people could *only* be saved by believing in him. White Eagle (my teacher) has given a slightly different interpretation: that people are saved by the Christ, the Son of God, the light within them, which shone so very brightly through Jesus. Jesus himself did not mean people to worship him; he knew he was being used by God to help the people of earth, as were all the teachers in this section, and many other saints and teachers of all religions throughout history.

Jesus' teaching was that of love and that we can make the 'Kingdom of God' come, here and now in our lives, not in the distant future. His most famous words are the Lord's Prayer (in which he explained how we should pray to God) and his summary of the ten commandments of Moses (see below, p. 24), 'Thou shalt love the Lord thy God with all thy heart, and with all thy soul, and with all thy mind, and with all thy strength: this is the first commandment. And the second is like, namely this, Thou shalt love thy neighbour as thyself. There is none other commandment greater than these.' (Mark 12: 30,31)

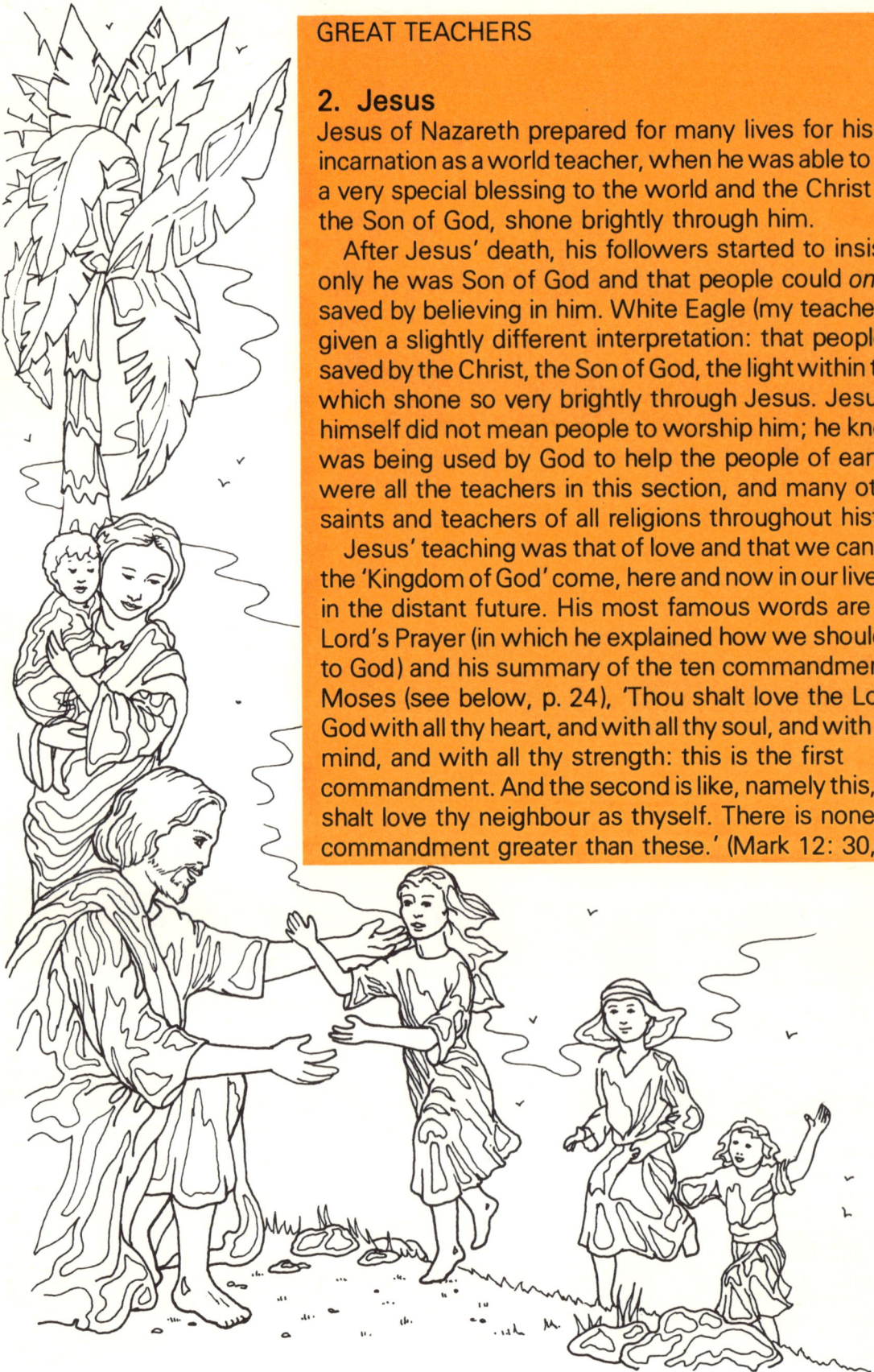

12

LUKE 24

His body vanished from his tomb and he appeared to Mary and the disciples. He showed us all that death of the body is not the end of life.

1

MY ABOUT BOOK JESUS

LUKE 2

Jesus was born in a stable in Bethlehem. Three wise men followed the Star to find him, and angels told shepherds where to look.

10

LUKE 22

The Last Supper with his disciples

3

MATTHEW 4

Jesus was tempted in the wilderness by the Devil. The wilderness symbolises the material world and the Devil symbolises our lower, selfish side.

8 Jesus healed many sick people, because the light of

God shone so brightly in him.

5

MATTHEW 6–7

In the Sermon on the Mount Jesus taught many things. For example, 'Not everyone that saith unto me, Lord, Lord, shall enter into the kingdom of heaven, but he that doeth the will of my Father'.

9

MY BOOK ABOUT JESUS (see overleaf)

2 | **11**

MATTHEW 3

When Jesus was baptised by John the Baptist, a dove appeared and God's voice said 'This is my beloved Son, in whom I am well pleased'.

LUKE 23

Jesus was crucified and even then he said 'Father, forgive them; for they know not what they do'. But he did not really die. . . .

4. Jesus chose twelve disciples to be his special

MARK 1

helpers. Their names were Simon Peter, Andrew, Philip, Nathanael, two called James, John, Thomas, Simon the Zealot, Judas Lebbeus and Judas Iscariot.

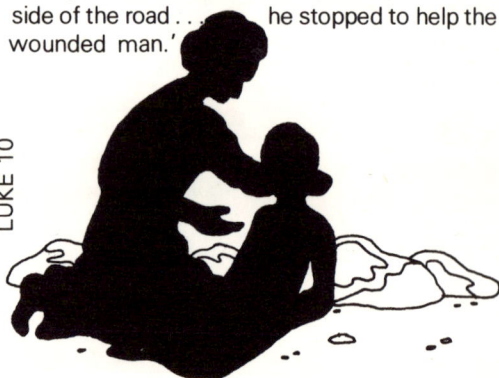

'The good Samaritan did not pass by on the other side of the road . . . . . he stopped to help the wounded man.'

9

LUKE 10

Jesus told stories, called parables, to teach his followers.
We can all be good Samaritans.

6 | **7**

MARK 6

Jesus performed miracles like feeding the five thousand people out of five loaves and two fishes.

MARK 5

Jesus walked on the water and calmed the sea. We can learn to 'calm the sea' of our emotions by keeping centred in the light.

GREAT TEACHERS

Jesus

PRAYER AND MEDITATION
Try to feel the presence of this beloved teacher as you say
the words (reprinted from the book of prayers by my
mother, Joan Hodgson, called OUR FATHER).

Dear Jesus, shining like the sun,
Whose light pours down on everyone,
I know there shines in my heart too
A light which draws me close to you.

As I softly say your name
It quickens to a lovely flame.
My guardian angel still and bright
Now shelters me in wings of light.

His wings build me a shining place
Where I can meet you face to face.
They shut out every earthly noise
Till I can hear your gentle voice.

Dear Jesus, through God's glorious light
You made men well – restored their sight,
Walked on the water, calmed the sea,
Fed hungry crowds in Galilee.

Dear Jesus, please come close to me,
You are my friend, help me to see
That God's pure light which shines through you
Is blazing now in my heart too.

It fills my body, heart and mind;
It helps to make me brave and kind;
It shines in everything I do
And helps me to grow more like you.

11

Buddha

3. Buddha

Siddhartha Gautama Buddha was born a prince in India in 563 BC. He was brought up in a palace surrounded by luxury. Because of a prophecy about what would happen if he saw anyone sick, old or dead, or a holy man, his father the king, tried to keep him from seeing what life is really like, allowing him only to see beauty and happiness. But when he was thirty the prophecy came true and he saw people suffering, and then a holy man, who was very calm and peaceful in spite of the suffering. He was no longer content and left his family, his palace and wealth to search out the meaning of life and death and suffering.

At first he followed a very severe path, nearly starving himself to death, but then he realised the 'middle path' is better, not having too much, nor too little. One day, during a long meditation (lasting seven days) in which he remembered many of his past lives, he received his great awakening and became BUDDHA – the enlightened one. Then he spent the rest of his life helping others understand 'The Four Noble Truths' and follow 'The Noble Eightfold Path'.

THE FOUR NOBLE TRUTHS
The suffering of physical life
The cause of suffering (self-desire and self-will)
The end of suffering (overcoming self-desire and self-will)
Nirvana (or freedom from all suffering and self-desire by following the Noble Eightfold Path).

THE NOBLE EIGHTFOLD PATH
1. Right understanding
2. Right thought
3. Right speech
4. Right action
5. Right living
6. Right effort
7. Right remembrance
8. Right meditation

Buddha

A PICTURE FOR YOUR ROOM
Colour and mount on card. Cut off this bottom panel to make a card prop
for your picture

Fold

Stick to
back of
picture

PLAY THE 'BUDDHA'S STEPPING STONES' GAME
Make eight stepping stones out of card with Buddha's
eight steps written on them and lay them out on the floor.
Play some music and dance round. When the music
stops, all stand on a stepping stone. Anyone not on a
stone is out. Whoever is on stone 1 says what his stone
means. Then remove this stone and continue the music.
Next time whoever is on stone 2 says what it means and
so on. The child left on stone 8 is the winner.

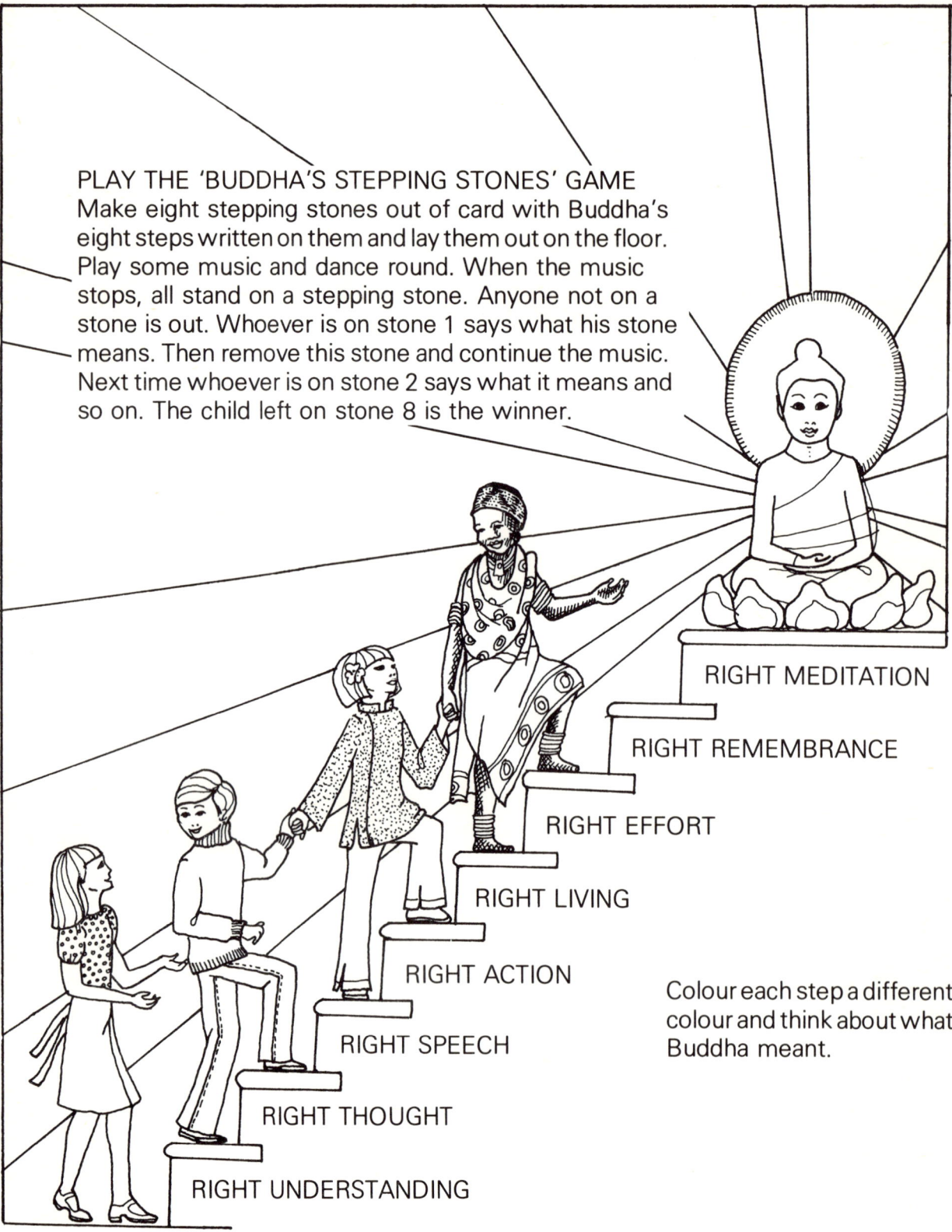

RIGHT MEDITATION

RIGHT REMEMBRANCE

RIGHT EFFORT

RIGHT LIVING

RIGHT ACTION

Colour each step a different
colour and think about what
Buddha meant.

RIGHT SPEECH

RIGHT THOUGHT

RIGHT UNDERSTANDING

14

MEDITATION

Here are two sayings of Buddha from the DHAMMAPADA.

'If a man when young and strong does not arise and strive when he should arise and strive, and thus sinks into laziness and lack of determination, he will never find the path of wisdom.'

'A man should control his words and mind and should not harm with his body. If these ways of action are pure he can make progress on the path of the wise.'

Think about the beauty and truth in these sayings. Sit quietly cross-legged or in the lotus position and picture a little flame of light. As you become more and more peaceful, the flame flickers less and less. You feel more and more peaceful, and love and light shine from your heart to all life.

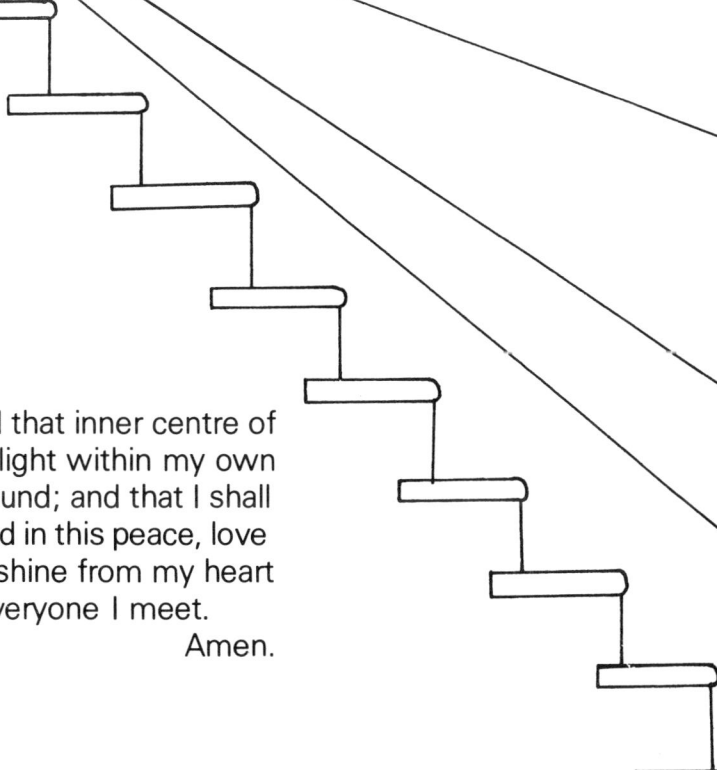

PRAYER

I pray that I shall find that inner centre of love and peace and light within my own heart that Buddha found; and that I shall one day be so centred in this peace, love and light, that it will shine from my heart to touch and help everyone I meet.

Amen.

4. Krishna

Krishna was born in India about 3000 BC. When he was a baby he spent all his time singing and dancing with the Gopis, the milkmaids. He was always smiling and happy, and full of joy and laughter.

When he grew up and saw that others were not happy he spent many years experiencing the pain and suffering of others to find out why. Finally, in a forest hermitage, he met a great Rishi (a spiritual teacher) who explained to him that all life is one. Everything from the lowest insect to the greatest king is part of the same life, part of God, and the reason why people are unhappy is that they do not realise this in their hearts. The Rishi also told Krishna that he had a very special mission, which was to bring this knowledge to other people by the example of his own life. Krishna did this and many people in India followed him on the joyful path. Nowadays he is loved by many Indian children in the way that Jesus is in the Western world.

The teachings of Krishna, which were given to his beloved disciple, Arjuna, are contained in a book called the BHAGAVAD GITA (an important book in the world's literature, like the Bible), which means 'The Lord's Song'. Krishna is always shown dancing and playing the flute, as he brings joy and happiness into our hearts.

Krishna

A PICTURE FOR YOU TO COLOUR

KRISHNA'S HAPPY MASK

Krishna dances and plays his flute to make us happy. Do you go around looking sad and making others sad, or looking happy and cheering them up? Here's a happy mask to make. It will remind you to smile and let your light shine.

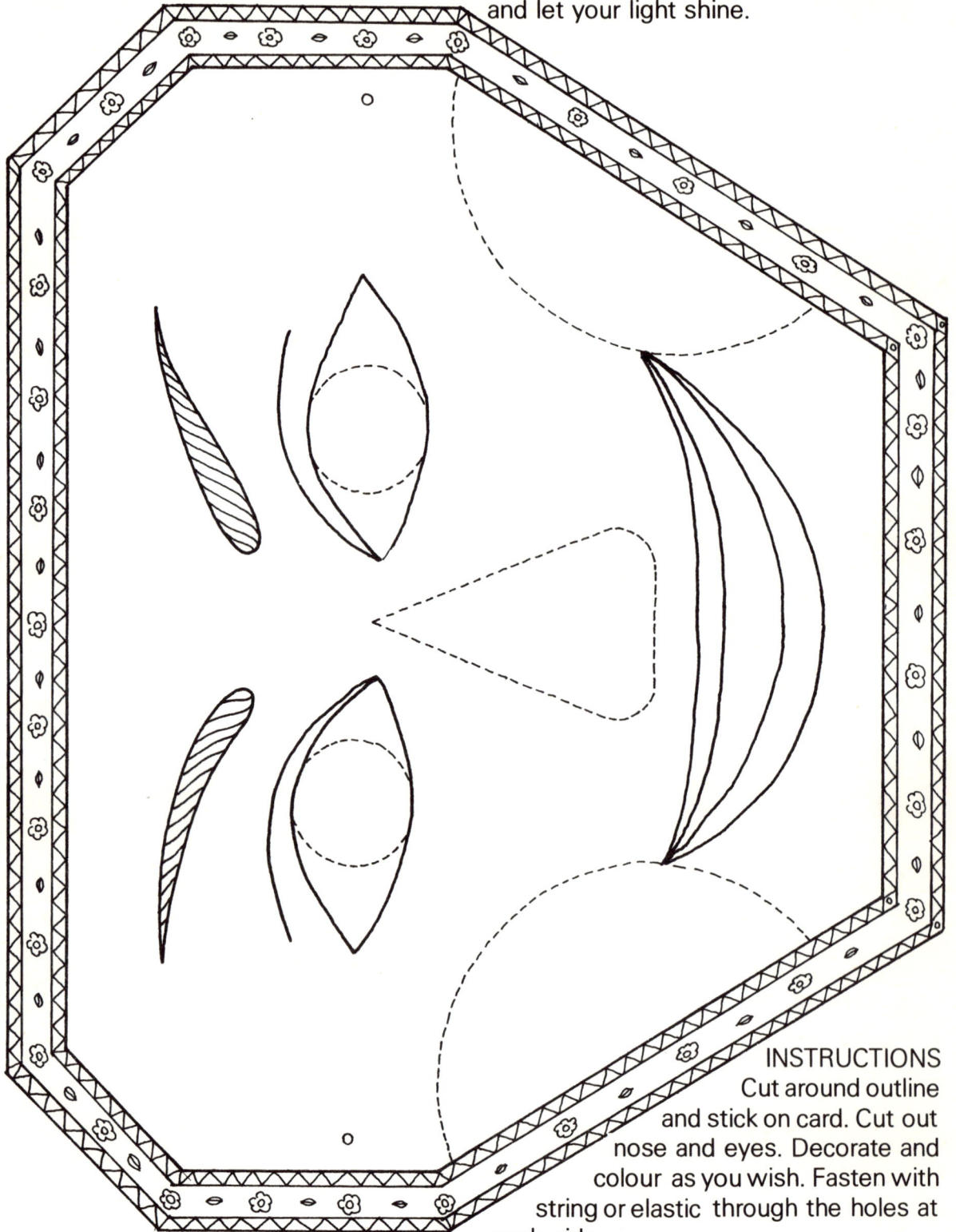

INSTRUCTIONS

Cut around outline and stick on card. Cut out nose and eyes. Decorate and colour as you wish. Fasten with string or elastic through the holes at each side.

GREAT TEACHERS

4. Krishna

MEDITATION

Think about this saying of Krishna's from the BHAGAVAD GITA.

'When we surrender all desires that come to the heart and by the grace of God find the joy of God, then our souls have indeed found peace.'

The secret of peace and happiness lies in letting go all our own ideas of what we want for ourselves, for other people and for the world, and accepting God's way, allowing His love and light to fill our hearts and minds.

As you sit quietly thinking about this, picture a pure white lily, a lotus flower, floating on a clear pool. It gradually opens in the light of the sun, and in its centre is a shining jewel.

Concentrate on the jewel, as you breathe in and out in slow, gentle rhythm. Try to feel that with every inbreath you are being drawn closer and closer to the jewel, the heart of the lotus, and becoming more and more in harmony with God's will and His love and light in all creation.

PRAYER

Lord of all life, I surrender all the desires that come to my heart, and pray that your light will so fill my whole being that I shall become a centre of your love, peace, joy and wisdom from this day on.

Amen.

5. Mohammed

Mohammed is the founder of the great world religion called Islam.

He was born in Mecca (in present day Saudi Arabia) in 570 AD. Both his parents died when he was young and he was brought up by his uncle, a merchant in Mecca, where at that time people believed in many 'gods' and that the way to please them was to kill animals in holy places! But as Mohammed grew up, he met people who were Christians and Jews and became convinced that there was one God of all people. He started to meditate on his own in a quiet cave away from the noise of Mecca. Then one day he heard a voice saying, 'You are the Messenger of Allah (God)'. During further meditations he saw the Angel Gabriel, and was given many messages from God. These were written down by his friends (with whom he shared what was happening) and were eventually put into a book called the KORAN (the bible of Islam).

Mohammed told people that they must submit to the will of Allah. Islam means the inner peace which comes when one does this, and more and more people joined the new religion.

Sufi teachers interpret the KORAN from an inner spiritual point of view, showing how to find God within the heart, and revealing the oneness of all life.

GREAT TEACHERS
Mohammed

PILGRIMAGE TO MECCA GAME
Regular prayer at the five appointed times is an important duty each day for Muslims, as is a pilgrimage to the holy city of MECCA at least once in a lifetime.

Colour and cut out prayer mats and use as counters in the dice game

MECCA
Holy City of
Islam
(END)

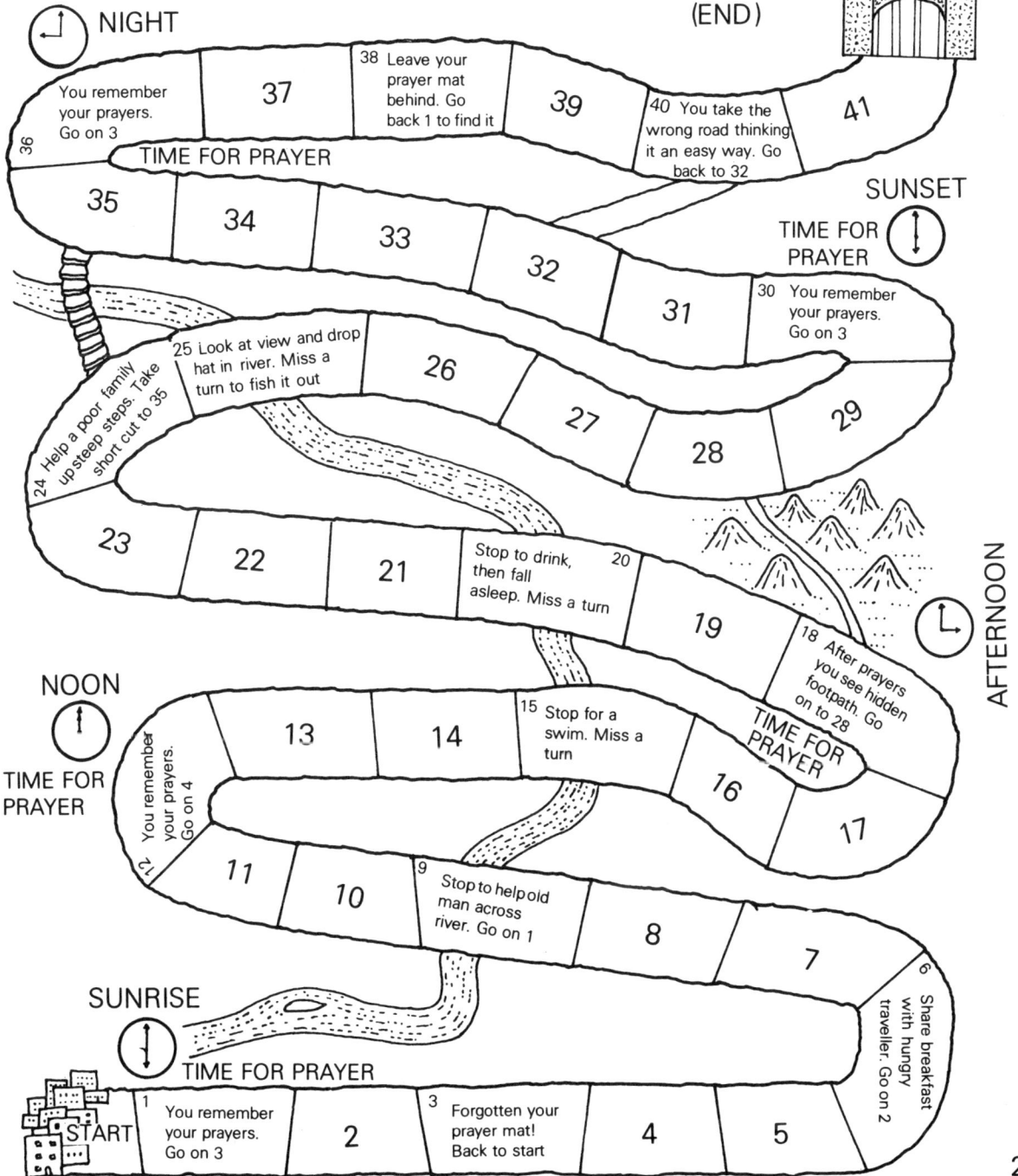

NIGHT

You remember your prayers. Go on 3

36

37

38 Leave your prayer mat behind. Go back 1 to find it

39

40 You take the wrong road thinking it an easy way. Go back to 32

41

TIME FOR PRAYER

SUNSET

TIME FOR PRAYER

35

34

33

32

31

30 You remember your prayers. Go on 3

24 Help a poor family up steep steps. Take short cut to 35

25 Look at view and drop hat in river. Miss a turn to fish it out

26

27

28

29

23

22

21

Stop to drink, then fall asleep. Miss a turn 20

19

18 After prayers you see hidden footpath. Go on to 28

AFTERNOON

NOON

TIME FOR PRAYER

12 You remember your prayers. Go on 4

13

14

15 Stop for a swim. Miss a turn

TIME FOR PRAYER

16

17

11

10

9 Stop to help old man across river. Go on 1

8

7

6 Share breakfast with hungry traveller. Go on 2

SUNRISE

TIME FOR PRAYER

START

1 You remember your prayers. Go on 3

2

3 Forgotten your prayer mat! Back to start

4

5

21

THE FIVE PILLARS OF ISLAM
Colour each pillar differently and think about its meaning

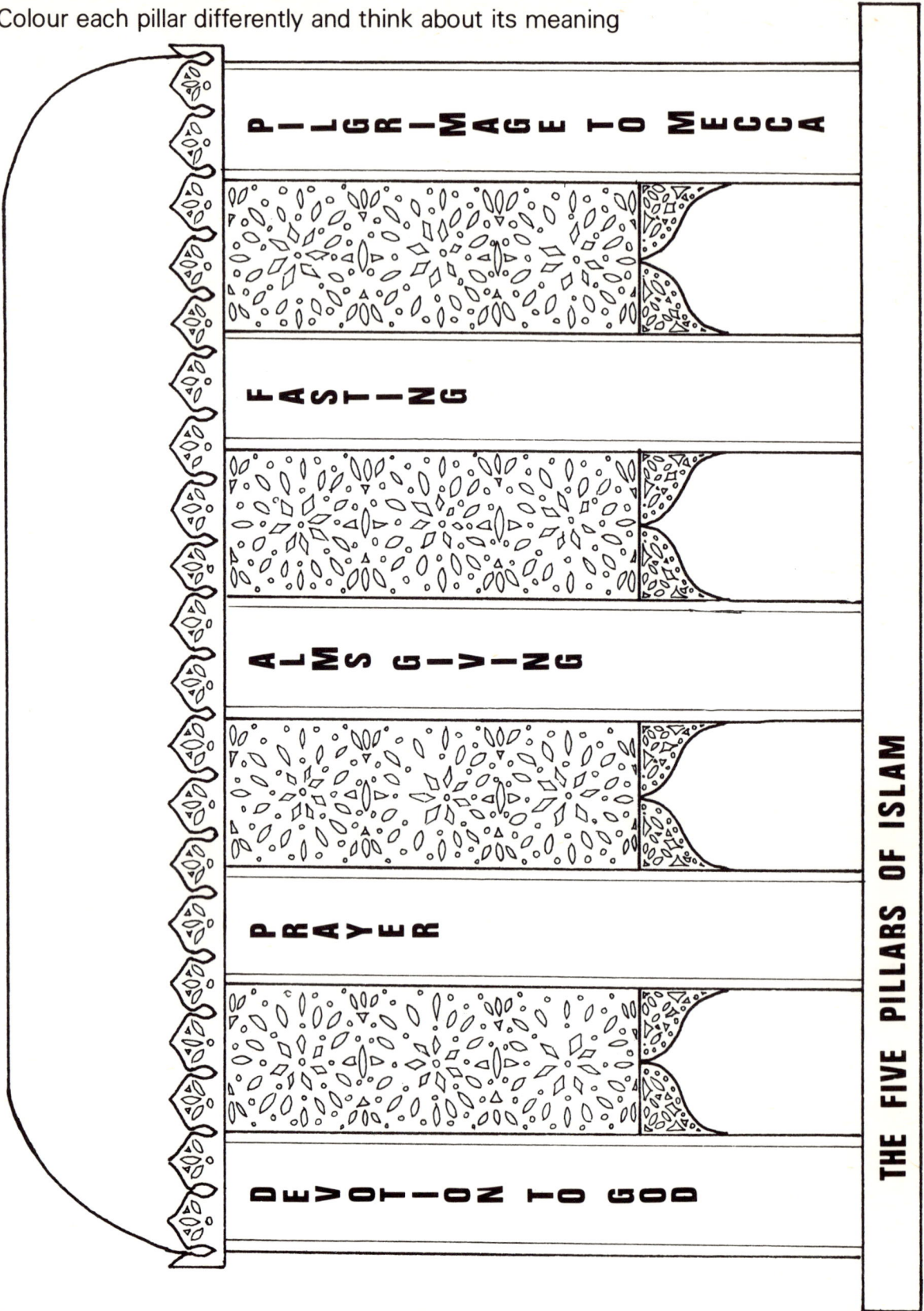

PILGRIMAGE TO MECCA

FASTING

ALMS GIVING

PRAYER

DEVOTION TO GOD

THE FIVE PILLARS OF ISLAM

GREAT TEACHERS
Mohammed

THE PILLARS OF ISLAM

1. A Muslim must recite the Creed of Islam. Every day he says 'La ilaha illa Allah, wa Muhammad rasula Allah': there is no God but Allah and Mohammed is the apostle of Allah.
2. A man (called the Muezzin) calls a Muslim to prayer (from the minaret of the mosque – their church) five times a day at dawn, noon, afternoon, evening and night.
3. A Muslim must fast in the month of Ramadan.
4. A Muslim must give alms (the KORAN states a fortieth of his money) – the idea is that a Muslim must share Allah's gifts with his brothers.
5. A Muslim must make a pilgrimage to Mecca once in his life.

MEDITATION AND PRAYER

Think about these five pillars and the truth which lies within them: absolute devotion to God, regular prayer, sharing, learning to control the physical appetite through fasting, making a real effort for the cause you believe in. We can all learn from them.

The KORAN begins with this prayer:

IN THE NAME OF ALLAH, THE COMPASSIONATE, THE MERCIFUL,
Praise be to Allah, Lord of the Creation,
The Compassionate, the Merciful,
King of Judgment-day!
You alone we worship, and to You alone we pray for help,
Guide us to the straight path,
The path of those whom You have favoured,
Not of those who have incurred Your wrath,
Nor of those who have gone astray.

6. Moses

The story of Moses is told in the Old Testament of the Bible. When all Hebrew babies were ordered to be killed by the wicked Pharaoh, Moses was hidden in the rushes of the Nile, and found by the Pharaoh's daughter.

When he grew up he became aware of God talking to him. In the story we read that this first happened when he saw a great fire in the bush, but the flames did not burn anything. He knew he had to lead his people, called the children of Israel, out of Egypt (where they were cruelly treated as slaves) to safety in the promised land.

Before they could leave Egypt many plagues and terrible things happened (brought about by God, so the story goes, to make the Pharaoh let them leave). These are symbols of the tests and difficulties we have to face in earth life. When they did escape from Egypt, they wandered for a long time in the wilderness (a symbol of caring only about worldly, selfish things). But when they were hungry God sent 'manna' to eat (the spiritual food God always gives His children).

During this time Moses was called to the top of Mount Sinai to receive from God the tablets of the Law, the ten commandments. When he came down he found his people worshipping a golden calf (symbol of material things), having forgotten about God (Jehovah, as they called Him). Moses was so upset he broke the tablets. But later he went up the mountain again and after forty days and forty nights, returned with new tablets and his people eventually did all the things they were told. Just before Moses died, aged over one hundred and twenty years, he was shown 'the Promised Land' to which he had so faithfully led his people.

Moses leads the children of Israel out of Egypt and makes a magical pathway through the Red Sea

MAKE A FRIEZE ABOUT MOSES' LIFE
Colour the little pictures which illustrate scenes from Moses' life. Cut them out and stick on a long strip of paper to make a frieze for your bedroom wall. Add some more pictures and background scenery.

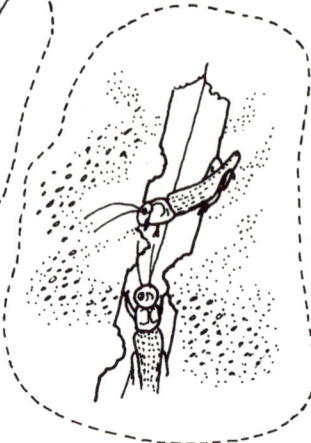

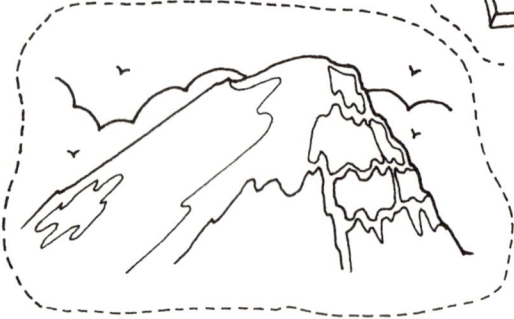

Stick the titles under the correct picture

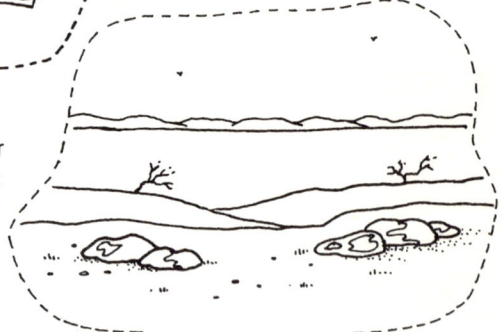

THE PROMISED LAND – a symbol of the heavenly world we can all find	THE PLAGUES – symbols of the many tests earth life brings	THE LAND OF EGYPT Pyramids are symbols of aspiration to God	THE GOLDEN CALF Symbol of material things
THE TABLETS OF THE LAW God's spiritual law for life on earth and in heaven	MOUNT SINAI We can learn to ascend the mountain in aspiration to God	THE BURNING BUSH We can all learn to hear God's voice in our hearts	THE WILDERNESS – symbol of a life based only on material things.

Moses

The story of Moses has a great deal of inner meaning (like many of the stories in the Bible) and we can learn many things if we hunt for the secrets. It really is like a treasure hunt! I have pointed out some clues but maybe you will spot more.

Let's think about the inner meaning of the ten commandments (Look up Exodus 20: 1–17). They really mean we must learn to love God (or good) more than anything else, more than all earthly things, and keep a regular time to meditate and pray. Secondly they give rules to help people behave in a kind and brotherly way to one another. Jesus summed up the ten commandments in his famous words about love (see Mark 12: 30–31).

Jews (the descendants of the 'children of Israel') try to put what they see as God's law (the Torah) into practice through their lives. They believe that by following the law with a pure heart and giving devotion to God in prayer, one can be directly in touch with God. They say this prayer in Hebrew each morning and evening:

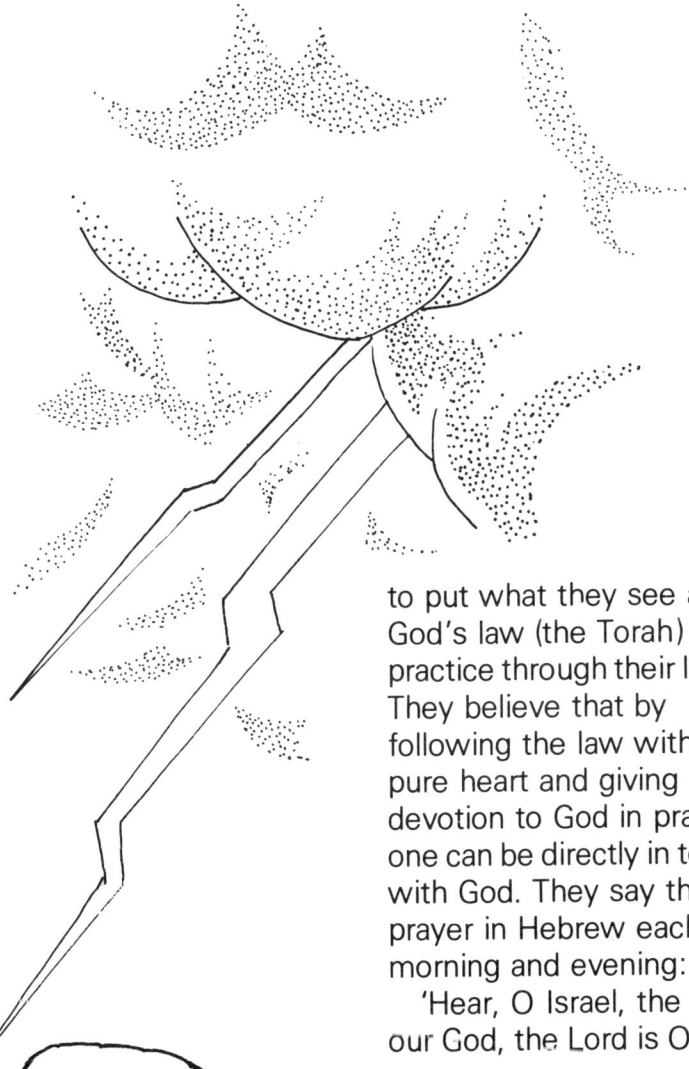

'Hear, O Israel, the Lord our God, the Lord is ONE'.

MEDITATION
Sit quietly and picture Moses climbing up the mountain in the sunlight to receive the Law from God. Think of the inner meaning of this story . . . we can all climb the 'mountain' of truth in our meditations and find God and learn about His law for life on earth.

7. Chinese philosophers

Lao-Tzu and Confucius

Lao-Tzu is 'the old philosopher' and lived in China from about 604 BC to 524 BC. As a child he learned about the Tao, the way of the universe. 'When everyone goes along with Tao', his teacher told him, 'the world is at peace and everyone is happy'. Lao-Tzu saw that many people did not understand or do this, and he wrote a book to help them called TAO TE CHING – THE BOOK OF THE RIGHT WAY. Later, in 4 BC, a scholar Chuang Tzu read Lao-Tzu's book and explained belief in the Tao in a way more people could understand, in a famous book which is called CHUANG TZU after him.

Confucius lived in China at about the same time as Buddha was alive in India. He tried to teach people how to behave so they could all live happily; he advised the governors of the Chinese states and even the emperor how they should rule. 'The trouble is', he said, 'everyone lives without paying attention to anyone else', and he suggested simple rules of

human kindness for everyone to follow, with special emphasis on family love and loyalty. He and others also collected all the stories and wise sayings of old China into books called the Chinese Classics. The I CHING, or Book of Changes, is the first of these and is one of the most important books in the world's literature, like the Bible, the BHAGAVAD GITA and the KORAN.

Zen

Zen has grown from Chinese philosophy merging with the teaching of Buddha. It has been practised in Japan since about AD 1200. Zen students seek complete understanding of all creation (like Buddha's sudden awakening to truth) through discipline of mind and body. Enlightenment can come whilst doing ordinary everyday tasks. Zen masters teach their pupils by using strange riddles called KOANS. These are designed to stop the ordinary thoughts of the physical brain, so the higher mind and intuition can reveal the truth. It often happens suddenly, in a flash of inner understanding. Here is a famous KOAN – when a monk asked the Zen Master, Joshu, what the principle of Buddha's teaching was he said 'the cypress tree in the courtyard'.

GREAT TEACHERS
Chinese philosophers

THE BOOK OF CHANGES (I CHING.) The I Ching is based on sixty-four six-lined diagrams called hexagrams (see next page). Each represents something in life, a feeling or a situation. They show the constant change and movement in life, and how everything can be transformed if one lives in harmony with the Tao, the way of God. They are used by some people for getting guidance and for meditation.

For instructions to HEXAGRAM GAME, see over

The grid below is a sheet of game cards, each showing a yin-yang symbol and a phrase. The phrases appearing across the columns are:

- YIN AND YANG
- Life does not stay the same, it is always changing
- To find happiness, we must be centred in God's love,
- balanced between opposites
- We need to accept the ebb and flow,
- growth and decay, in life

HEXAGRAM GAMES

GAME 1. Cut out the cards and turn them all hexagram side down. Take it in turns to turn two over. If they match keep them and score one point. If they don't, turn them down again. Go on until all cards are paired.

GAME 2. Lay out a number of cards, face up, all different. (Use only six to start with.) Ask a grown-up to remove one. Now try and draw the missing hexagram. Score a point for each correct line. First player with 30 points wins.

ENTHUSIASM	CREATIVE	ENTHUSIASM	CREATIVE
UNEXPECTED	RECEPTIVE	UNEXPECTED	RECEPTIVE
WATER	DIFFICULTY	WATER	DIFFICULTY
FIRE	WAITING	FIRE	WAITING
FAMILY	CONFLICT	FAMILY	CONFLICT
KEEPING STILL	PEACE	KEEPING STILL	PEACE

GREAT TEACHERS

Chinese Philosophers

MEDITATION

Life does not stay the same, it is always changing. To find happiness we need to stay centred in God's love, perfectly balanced between the two opposites (called by the followers of the Tao YIN and YANG), accepting the natural ebb and flow, growth and decay in all life.

Chuang Tzu says:
'In the transformation and growth of all things, every bud and feature has its proper form. In this we have their gradual maturing and decay, the constant flow of transformation and change.'

Huai Nan Tzu says:
'Those who follow the natural order flow in the current of the Tao'.

Lao-Tzu says:
'Without going out of this door, man can know the universe; without looking out of his window, man can perceive the heavenly Tao'.*

Think about these sayings and then picture the sun shining on the sea and watch the gentle ebb and flow of the waves. They never stay still, but within the movement is stillness and peace for the movement is natural and in harmony with the Tao, the Creator's law of life. Thank you, our Creator, for the eternal beauty of life lived in harmony with you.

*This saying is like a riddle: do you know the answer? It means that every man has God in his heart and is a part of all creation, so through the God within his own self he can learn everything.

THE 'SPIRITUAL TEACHING

God loves us all   1

Help your children learn about our Creator and the brotherhood of all life. A book with meditations and prayers to awaken the understanding and experience of the love of God, as shown in the beauty of the created world; and to encourage the light in the heart to shine, and so bless and heal. Play-as-you-learn activities include making a shining star brooch, a novel 'busy mother' wheel, a fairy mobile and even a wriggling 'Mr Curly-Wurly Worm'. Children from all over the world are shown in the pictures.

Illustrated with colour overlay by Christina Marsh

32pp, wire-stitched   **£1.75**
ISBN 0 85487 051 2   (by post £2.00/ US$3.25)

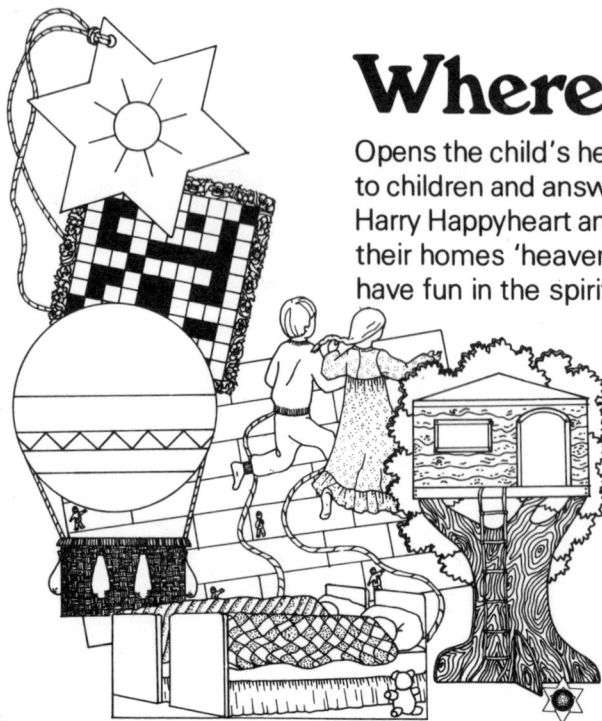

ALL FOUR IN THE SERIES AVAILABLE AS A SET AT SPECIAL PRICE OF £6.75 (BY POST £7.25/US$11.95)

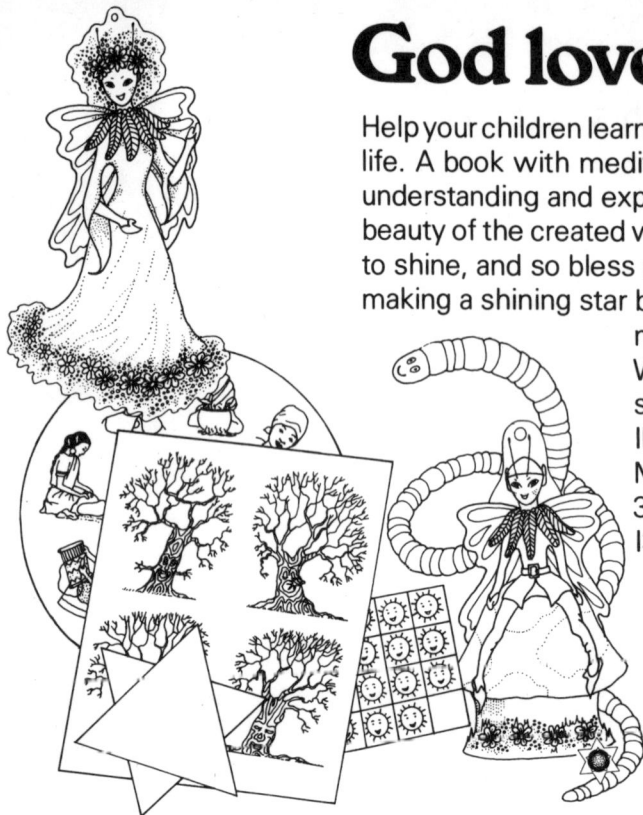

Where is Heaven?   2

Opens the child's heart and mind to the spirit world. Explains death to children and answers their questions about life after death. Meet Harry Happyheart and Crispin Crosspatch and learn how they make their homes 'heaven' and 'hell', and visit Peter and Penny as they have fun in the spirit world (a cut-out game to play). Make a magic sunshine wheel and a little book of your own. And in quieter moments use the meditations and prayers to experience the reality of the heaven world.

Illustrated with colour overlay by Christina Marsh

32pp, wire-stitched   **£1.75**
ISBN 0 85487 052 0   (by post £2.00/ US$3.25)